Fit For Human Consumption

Ian Walton

Acknowledgements

Some of these poems have previously appeared in other publications:

Orbis, Envoi, Literary Review, Pause, Blind Defiance Anthology, First Impressions Anthology, Envoi Anthology, The Journal of The Society of Teachers of Speech and Drama.

First published in Great Britain in 1991 by Poetry Now

Copyright Ian Walton 1991
1st printed in 1991 by Orton Graphics
2nd Edition 1992 Forward Press - Peterborough
3rd Edition 1992 Forward Press - Peterborough
4th Edition 1994 Forward Press - Peterborough
5th Edition 2008 Forward Press - Peterborough
6th Editon 2015 Spiderwize - Peterborough

Contents

Parlour Games

There is a look it's better to ignore:
a whisper in the eye, a sideward glance
designed to steal the heart and gently draw
those half breathed sighs that make the maybes dance.

There is a touch it's safer to deny:
an accidental brush against the skin,
an artful stroke that makes you wonder why
it leaves the smell of stranger, lingering.

There is a voice it's wiser not to hear:
a siren's breath that carries from the sea
the words unspoke, unsaid, that you most fear,
the cryptic code of lovers yet to be.

But if you should resist, you know the cost:
a lifetime's longing for a moment lost.

Some Circumstantial Evidence . . .

For seventeen days
he found
a trout in his milk

yet still believed her
when she
told him it was pure.

Marking Time

He is eighty-four:
scarred survivor
of a young man's bed;
two marriages;
an old man's war;
a brief affair;
a wild encounter
with a whore
in Paris, France.

She is fifteen,
still in white socks,
pride of the cavalcade,
tossing her staff, oblivious
to the stiff parade
that lines the Cenotaph:
erect, with red lapels,
giving two minutes worth of life
to those who fell;
to those who 'almost live'
and well remember Paris, France.

He sees her pass:
plump cheeks beat out
the rhythm of the drum.
Beneath his coat, marking time,
cold fingers shrive
old battle scars, inflicted
by a long-dead comrade's wife
in Paris, France.

It is remembrance day.

I Taught Her

I taught her how to smile:
she laughed at me.

I taught her how to talk:
she shouted at me.

I taught her how to walk:
she ran away.

De Intus

The many things I could have done that might
have helped. The times I said 'I will' but then
I raised myself above my fellow men
and chose to walk the darker side of night
accepting fame and fortune: the delight
of gladly seeking peers amongst a den
of thieves and hoping to deceive him when
I know there's nothing hidden from his sight.

With silent strokes the Reaper calls and leaves
the winnowed chaff upon the thresher's floor:
the meagre harvest of a season's sin.
I take my place with vagabonds and reeves
and though I stand, a stranger, at his door
I know he will forgive and ask me in.

Haiku

Peeled paint; twisted boards:
fingers fondle splintered wood.
Sun sets on white sails.

Shortest Day

At 12.01, July the 5th, he cried
soft silent tears of unremitting pain
At 12.02, July the 5th, he tried

to shift his weight a little but, denied
the use of limbs, all effort was in vain.
At 12.09, July the 5th, he cried

a dry-spit croak; alone, and terrified
of death while others slept, he croaked again.
At 12.14, July the 5th.he tried

to hold his bowels: last vestige of his pride
dissolving as he felt his body wane.
12.17, July the 5th, he cried

a final scream that brought her to his side,
and smelling blood she smiled down with disdain.
12.22, July the 5th, he tried

to bare a soul that countless fathers hide:
words dripped, impotent, on the counterpane.
12.24, July the 5th, he cried:
12.26, July the 5th, he died.

Wave Goodbye

Dive.
White horses crash
against my bow.
Abandon ship.
Still waters call.

The Homecoming

Far away, at the limit of the eye
where sea and sky dissolve
into a turquoise haze,
her gaze, hangs.

In answer,
sail tips announce a safe return:
the fleet inches its way back
over the edge
and cleaves a passage home.

In line they wait:
black shawls and buckets.
Ribald laughter echoes from the dock,
(no blushes here),
practised cheers make fast the ropes.

A good catch:
blades flash in facile hands
as innards are despatched,
bodies dressed and packed.
Through narrow streets,
hung heavy with the smell of blood,
she cleaves a passage home;
trips on his boots
left by the door;
swears deep beneath her breath;
mounts the stair;
listens for the snore.
Eyes glazed,
she slips a hand between the sheets,
eviscerates the bloated gut
and cleans her knife once more.

Pebbles

The years
could have been kinder:
she finds herself alone.

Ankles locked
she drags her way back
to the fold
and hopes
to find redemption
from the sin
she sold on waterfronts
and piers . . .

. . . and she,
who often laid with Muslim,
and with Jew,
now rubs herself
on Wee-Free's splintered pew;
pricks her arse on piety
one day out of seven
to attain the promised pathway
through the needle eye
to Heaven.

Casts stones
at busty blondes
who work their patch,
(content to scratch a living
on the cocks
of lusty jacks);

sips tea,
refuses wine:
afraid one glass will turn
the withered hands of time back
to her past.

We meet,
this reformed Jezebel
and I.
I offer wine, explain:
salvation may be fine, but
surely
can be claimed
at any time
before the final hour.

Why waste a life?
Why waste a body?
Heaven will wait.

Heaven waits: once more she pounds
her beat along the shore
where countless rollers
knock her off
her feet.

Legs spread;
thighs locked;
half pissed;
half cocked;
with squeals of joy
(and fifteen quid)
she welcomes home
the fleet.

Any Way Up

Bingo caller,
kerb crawler
Eddie
said I talk
with a plum
in my mouth.
The bum!

He said I'm U
'cos when I screw
I don't chew my gum
like the other girls do.

I said,
'Stop taking the piss,
just gis a kiss,
and pull me vest down
when you're through!'

The Travelling Man

Size five, thin-strapped, sling-backed, brass-buckled shoes
swing languidly on red-tipped toes. High heels
provocatively invite him to choose
between the photograph and her. He feels
his way to the bar. Strawberry lips drip
practised whispers. Fingering his wife's face
in place behind his credit cards, he slips
out two notes: scarlet fingertips erase
three hundred miles of road, and thoughts of home.
They let the gin, and conversation, flow,
allowing eyes to linger. Fancies roam
as strangers play their game of touch-and-go.
    Deftly she glides him to her crimson light;
    turns back the sheets, puts him up for the night.

A Dangerous Thing

He knew
and burdened with the knowledge
daily grew more evil
until goodness shone
through his hollow eyes
drawing souls into their glow
and all men loved him
but he knew.

Russian Dolls

They lie in bed, afraid
to show their true deceit:
feather-pillow analysts who dared
to bare the centre of their lives;
their dreams.
Staring at their nakedness
each from the other fled
and wove new clothes.
Nightly, in each other's arms
they exorcise all thoughts
of paradise.

He places kisses on her neck,
swears his love
beneath the chiffon dress
his mother draped around his waist
while Daddy fought the Germans
for a place in history's cold marble
hall of fame.
She casts spells around his cock:
wishes it soft, subservient
to the female charms
perfected in her father's arms.

Both have almost seen the core,
recoiled and tasted fruit: he
spends his nights with movie queens: she
is hogged by rugby teams, and
to the outside world
it seems they'll love each other
till they die.
He knows;
she knows;
they both are dead
that's why they lie
in bed.

Chinese Takeaway

A million kids came out to play,
laughter echoed round the square.
The big boys took their toys away
and left the children lying there.

Last Tango In Tooting

As global warming took its grip
and passions rose with every tide,
mad dogs roamed the streets at noon:
inhibitions pushed aside,
daring all, we took the chance
to exorcise our temperance
and ventured to the office dance.

Dribbling libido down his leg,
a languid Latin tapped my arm;
wrapped himself around my wife;
whispered 'may I' and oozing charm
slid her across the polished boards,
between the tanned and tainted hordes
of Arab-Geordies from up north.

The band struck up in double time:
I stiffened as a paramour's
soft hand explored my inner thigh;
my wife was writhing on the floor
with a lizard of a man
(sporting a Llanelli tan)
who looked a lot like Genghis Khan.

The buffet stank of kiwi fruit
and melons grown in Inverness
that sun-kissed maids from Sutherland
proffered to guests. I must confess,
I had no reason to suspect
the ozoneless greenhouse effect
would propagate such wanton sex.

Unto Us A Child Is Born

Black, night black, behind low clouds
to the east
a star rises; creeps, silent:
advances.

Martyrs, crow-pecked, pave the streets
to the east
as his steel-grey entourage
advances

rolls forward crushing bone. Skulls
bleached: children
born old, kerbstone his pathway
to the east.

Prostrate; palm-leaved; his people
wait for him
to ride his ass, triumphant
to the east.

Open Invitation

'Well, it's like this, Mrs Branston:
the point of our inquiry,
of all these pointed questions,
is for us to determine
if there's grounds for us proceeding,
or, maybe there was an inkling
of encouragement forthcoming?
No! No need to be offended,
it's just, maybe without knowing,
you did something quite inviting
to that poor sod in the cells.'

'It's like this, Inspector English:
as I left the office party,
and walked quick, across the car park,
so as not to draw attention,
I could swear I saw a figure,
crouched behind a Ford Fiesta.
I could see a silver sliver:
a sharp dagger, thrust before him,
glinting gaily, in the moonlight.
So I ran towards the darkness,
and I threw myself upon him?

'It was difficult, believe me,
as we grappled on the tarmac.
Once or twice I almost lost him
as my fingers sought my knickers,
and I ripped the stockings from me,
and I pushed him deep inside me,
and I rained his fists upon me,
branding memories within me,
that will haunt me for a lifetime.
Then I laid me, still, beneath him,
suffocating in his kindness?'

'Well it's like this, Mrs Branston.'
'Don't interrupt me now Inspector!
I have difficulty talking
from the pain, that's a reminder,
of the boot so well directed,
by my hand, into my cheekbone,
as he stood astride me, laughing,
while I coaxed the urine from him,
pulling tight the silken stocking
round my neck, till interrupted,
by the sound of cars approaching.

So I lay there on the gravel,
and I dragged my skin across it,
weeping joy into a puddle
as I grovelled for forgiveness
from the men who get exited
by young women, walking homeward,
in the hours after darkness.
No, I should not feel offended:
because, maybe, without knowing,
I did something quite inviting
to that poor sod in the cells.'

Slag Heap (A Mills And Boon Romance)

Scarf tight against the shadow of the pit
she shuffles in scuffed heels
through cobbled streets
to keep a rendezvous
in Ishmail's corner shop
where wives and widows
stop to seek romance
in chance meetings
on a wire rack.

Lovers stacked on lovers revolve
in high-gloss covers, wrapped
round sixty thousand whispers, slipped
inside a bag for her
to carry home and fling
onto her bed.
Shedding shopping; coal-blacked clothes
and dignity
she pulls the curtains closed.

> She floats on bubbled words, a demimonde:
> craved, saved, then taken
> to the final page where hands
> stray and, idly, lay between her thighs.

> Fingers, playing, brush damp lips; she sighs
> savours the twist as, wantonly,
> she throws herself
> into her hero's arms.

The hooter mourns another shift. She
drags an eye up to the clock; feels him
seeping from the shaft; oozing home to cough
into her.

Square Peg

He was a big man:
North country.
Didn't mince his words:
Joe Blunt.

His opinions
could always
be relied upon.
Straight from

the shoulder he spoke
his mind and
seeing us at fault
told us.

Joe Blunt never changed
his mind: he
changed his world; kept it
pickled.

When he died I dug
Joe Blunt's grave:
very deep; a wide
round hole.

Poets Day (A Performance)

It is Friday, pm, early:
it is early, he feels horny.

Being Friday; feeling horny,
he has left the office, early:
left the early, burly doorman
standing by the double doors;

tidied up his desk and tried to
tidy up his tie, he tried to
tie with cool sophistication
after luncheon with young Gladys;
after Gladys; after luncheon.

. . . so he wanders, as a fishknife:
sharp as steel, hunting bonies;
finds a fillet he would fillet
flinging shopping in a trolley.

. . . so he takes her by the salad;
trips the aisle's terrazzo tiles
to the place where Tate and Lyle's
syrup's stacked above the piles . . .
she smiles.

He bends her over a gondola:
bends her like an uncoxed oarsman
dips his end into the water,
pulling oars in; ripple stroking,

strokes her nipples; nips her; strokes her;
dribbles spittle from his rowlocks.
There he has her in a manner
many men might never manage:
has her inside - insides outside -
by the checkout, inside Asda.

To Those Who Wait

We met, briefly;
you winked in summer's dress.
Ranks closed as I pressed you
tightly: testing.

For life you clung:
your cohorts battled
drawing blood.

I withdrew
for three weeks,
maybe four,
certainly no more.

We met, briefly.
One whispered caress
brought you leaping
from your ring of thorns.

Petrified

No royal pardon; plea for clemency
can save her now. Suspended overhead
- a steady dripping stalactite - he sheds
his icy drops of masculinity.
Transfixed, entombed in stone servility
she sees them spun into a crystal thread
that slowly binds her to his will. Drip-fed
on dreams, she fights instinctively.

Finally the day arrives for leaving,
she quietly packs her life into a case;
drags a bag of dreams towards the station
        - having nothing she thought worthwhile taking,
        and looking forward to the extra space -
hurries to an unknown destination.

Domical

Horizons move in concert
as eyes, hung on the edge,
inch along the precipice
where sea and sky infuse
their turquoise brew.

Above the eyrie
granite fingers, gloved in white,
poke fun at clouds
that fall on narrow roads.

Check,
take half a step:
watch horizons move
and on a clear day
reveal the dog-eared corners
of the world.

Domestic Appliance

My fridge is on the blink.
I think it is the thermostat:
keeps cutting out
then coming on again.

One minute it's fine:
keeps everything quite firm,
hard even. Then,
without warming,
butter's melting;
dripping
through the wire shelves.

I've adjusted the controls;
fiddled with the motor;
kicked it;
spent hours sitting around
waiting for it to cut out
then come back on again.

It's been serviced three times
by a man who seems to know
his stuff.
It went OK
for a week or two
but it was a high price to pay
when it still
keeps coming on
then cutting out
again.

There But For The Grace Of God

Four hundred million lemmings and one,
poised at the starting line
to sprint to Armageddon.

Four hundred million lemmings and one,
full of hope, racing blindly
towards their destination.

Four hundred million lemmings and one,
dreaming of eternal life
and you've condom.

Dear John

Some poets talk of shit on leeks; gaffe pike
in dusty reading rooms; spit consonants
at random rows of devotees: obliged
to pay lip-service to their annual grants.

While others, more exalted, throw their nets
into old libraries, and far below
the erudite meniscus trawl the depths
of 'Fowler's' hunting words, yet drag up 'crow'.

Wading thigh deep in lexicons, I cast
my own line, tempting couplets, unaware
that on the bank a shadow from the past
creeps by with poachers' stealth to raid a lair.

I feel the merest ripple as your slow
soft dappled, shirt-sleeved arm slips in the stream;
your gentle fingers play and even though
Myfanwy hides, you tickle out a dream.

Tilt

Hold tight,
walk with me
to lands where
footsteps ripple angels' tears
and fear is real;
every nail is counted;
numbered stones are fashioned into dreams
and thrown into the world . . .

      and we will dance on silver threads
      and leave the dead as carrion by the road.

She Tarzan

Dawn coughs;
spits her from the bed.
On shaky legs
she picks a path through soiled dreams;
scrapes away last night's remains;
draws deep
and dares herself
to fake another day.

Power dressed:
a double breasted amazon,
she rubs the hard crust from her eyes,
extends her stride and tries to catch
the passing body-tide.

By lunch, time synchronised, she struts
long-lashed, tight-thighed,
from powder rooms to exercise
her pelvic grip on fat cigars -
the very best the town's bars can provide.

Appetites are satisfied: glasses refilled.
A wayward hand is lifted from her leg,
led along the tablecloth,
placed on the spot and teased
to sign an autograph
across her order pad.

Bargain struck; sale made,
she powers home
her sixteen valve, two litre
central locking dick;
sheds her epiderm of graphic hype;
crawls back between the grubby sheets
she promised she would wash
a week last Wednesday.

The Parting

I will not go:
no spent and scrawny frame
claims my obeisance
from the grave.

I will resist
the grip of rawboned fingers,
pick them from my wrist
and crush the rimy hand
that never dared
to touch my cheek
with tenderness;
uncurl my long-clenched fist,
in which he pressed
his ice cream coins
of conscience,
wrap it round his withered neck,
shake out my life
and lay to rest
this bag of bones;
this man I never kissed
goodnight.

Poles Apart

As glasses clash:
ring out the private fears
he has of walking to Gethsemane,
the groom,
with courage born of revelry,
rears up: locks antlers
with another beer
while she,
across the town,
in cavalier disguise,
displays with pride a gartered knee;
in one sad act
of hot debauchery, against a wall,
off-loads her thin veneer.

On neutral ground they meet
and plight their troth.

Rings blessed; exchanged; knot tied
the separate halves unite
and in the sight of God are one.
Trawled families
congratulate them both.

The day consigned
to glossy photographs, they kiss;
lock limbs, and cross
the rubicon.

Pub Talk

Country's fucked:
recession
they call it
on the box.

Westminster live?
dead from the neck up,
I reckon.

They say
inflation
is the biggest enemy:
bigger than starvation;
malnutrition, or
lack of education.

They talk all day
of interest rates;
what interests me
is how to pay the tallyman
and still have a few quid over
to get pissed.

Flotsam

When in her company
he walked
two inches off the ground;
maintained an orbit,
not elliptical but,
perfectly round:
unmoved by outside forces.

They walked:
he walked two inches off the ground.
Her white-veiled innocence
helped to confound the principle
that brings the apple down.

Now, in her company, he walks
two inches off the ground
afraid the sound of stockinged-feet
might irritate.

Still he hovers,
treading love
while she, at random,
picks her morning gifts
unaware of his old body
bobbing
on the gently ebbing tide.

Thank Heaven

'Grow up,' she said
and led him
up the stairs
to her,
and father's
bed.

'Grow up,' she said.
He grew:
a strapping man
of ten.
Thirty years
have found him
now a boy
amongst the men,
reduced
to prowling streets
seeking satisfaction
with a bag
of boiled sweets.

Jetsam

Becalmed, they wait to die.

Storm lashed, mast splintered,
all ballast spent, mechanically
they bale
in a forlorn attempt to save
the leaking vessel.
> They sailed, full rigged,
> tacked to the sun
> failing only when their words,
> in the teeth of the fiercest gale,
> were lost.
They drift; water creeping up the bow:
in the prow she sleeps, he
shifts his weight astern, sees
that if one of them should be
thrown overboard
the boat would rise -
chances are the other would survive.

He weighs the proposition:
weighs his wife:
jettisons the shrivelled wreck
that threatens to destroy her life.

She stayed afloat: he struck out
in all directions.
She was rescued by a passing boat;
taken in tow
by the master of the craft.

Of him? I heard
they picked him from the rocks,
two weeks later, at low tide:
a passing shag had took his eyes; crabs
the best part of the rest.

Toes

You see
you don't know
the things that have to happen
once you tentatively dip your little toe
into the water.

One toe;
two toes;
on it goes until you're paddling
and will not end
until your wet and naked body's
straddling mine:
you see, I've found
one toe . . .
you drown.

Sheffield

. . . and so you blow your separate world,
high above malignant time.
Settling gently, now and then
to take aboard the family ties:
    father with his spastic hands,
    mother with her inane smile,
    sucklings taking life for life,
    husband, hog-like, at your crotch.
They take more than you can give,
and so you blow your separate world,
hide inside your spheroid dreams,
but find, with every passing year,
surface tension holds you in.
Until the separate world you blew
sets hard into a steel ball,
and all the elbows that you throw
cannot pierce the bubble's wail.

A Reciprocal Arrangement

What if the leaf knew
of the tree's naked mystery:
trembling through winter's lifeless days,
flexing knarled fingers,
clutching spring's first rays,
joy weeping from each dormant eye
exorcising monocarpic fears.

Would each dried leaf have hung
as autumn called,
tearless, waiting to be shed
or seized the day:
with one accord
let go.

What can the leaf know
of the tree
except to cling.

Colour Blind

The grip was firm, though feminine,
a nurse perhaps, and he,
not being overfond of dogs,
felt grateful for her hand.

She sat him down and quietly
explained that he had stumbled
on a 'private do', then asked
if he would stay.

They spoke at length:
she made no move to go.

He thought she must be fat;
glasses at least;
hare-lipped, or even
worse.

Then he caught a slightly
eastern smell: a hint of tamarind
as she whispered
'will you come again,'
he hesitated,
interpreting the signs
alarms ringing, searching
for a dialect in a sigh:
a nigger on the wind.

He touched her cheek
and tried to feel
the colour of her skin.

Lorraine ROP

Inside the chase
a teenage bride
lies dead.
Her death, italicised
in quotes
of twelve point molten lead
cast cold into a marble bed,
is proofed
then passed by carnal eyes
of vultures who immortalise
in em spaced rows,
that sexualise a husband's grief,
the truth that's shred
inside the chase.

Prearranged,
to patronise rich marketeers,
who advertise their world
amongst the stories
spread across the page
in columns fed on blood,
bold letters eulogise
inside the chase.

A Word To The Wise

Unnoticed as the silver moon
that slips into the winter sky,
in stealth, she crept throughout the land
and poisoned every drinking hole.

All the people in the land
drank deeply from the river's depths
and all the people in the land awoke
and all the land was crazed.

All the land save one: the king
who drank not from the water's edge
but from the spring that underground
flows hidden from her tainted breath.

All the people in the land
they cried, 'Alas, the king is mad.
The king is mad. The king is mad.
The king is mad: God save the king.'

In the night the king arose.
Afraid the crowd might cast him out
he stumbled to the river bank,
plunged his hands into the deep
and brought them, trembling, to his lips.

All the people in the land
they cried, 'Rejoice, the king is saved.
The king is saved. The king is saved.
The king is saved.'

God save the king.

It Is Finished

Tears were in fashion,
young men bought young guitars,
starlight kissed us:
life peers.

It's over, gone.
Blinkered bus-talk, designer duffles.
Painted playmats tossed into the bin.
Starlight kissed us,
a generation of strangers
hung between the devil and our children;
picking up the phone and listening in.

Last night no tears would fall:
tears are out of fashion.
501's, visa, hi-tech state of the art:
Big bang.

It's over: gone.
Old men finger old guitars.
We were kissed by starlight;
such a brief kiss.

Fairy Rings

Coming dear.
Yes, coming dear.
Yes dear! I've washed my hands.

In mountain streams where tickled trout,
soft shadows by the bank,
play lazily with death
he washed his hands.

On battlefields
where devils meet
and broken souls wait patiently
to die,
he wiped his feet;
carved his meat
in banquet halls
where victors dine as kings;
made his bed in palaces
where soft young shadows
at his feet
wait lazily for death . . .

and windmills fell
and dragons flew
and nails pierced his hands.

In oaken glades, by mountain streams
in far off lands, on summer nights
in fairy rings he sat . . .

Coming dear.
Yes, coming dear.
Yes dear! I've fed the cat.

Triptukhos

Always there is three.
Singular and plural
have their trinity and ternary.

Always there are three:
 the love with it
 that shows its head
 to newlyweds, caressing stars
 into their dreams.

 The love of it
 that breeds the marl-marked stripper:
 brings the ripper, sobbing,
 to the bar.

 The love for it:
 the standard bearers' cries,
 detached, seducing death to a decision.

The two of us,
knarled together.
The three of us
embracing the three of them.

Shepherd's Pie

The whores of Rome and London are to blame
for every brother broken by despair;
every spastic hero's act of shame.

For 'God is mine', for claim and counterclaim:
power, pretended, that they fight to share,
the whores of Rome and London are to blame.

For every bomb - salvation in the flame -
for every kneecap shattered in their snare;
every spastic hero's act of shame,

for every horror bullets may contain;
every nail scattered on a prayer,
the whores of Rome and London are to blame.

For every helpless, hopeless heart they maim;
every soldiers-bastard's shaven hair;
every spastic hero's act of shame;

every mother widowed in God's name;
every cripple sentenced to the chair:
the whores of Rome and London are to blame
for every spastic hero's act of shame.

Cutting Edge

Ice maiden
dance a pirouette
on virgin crystals
cold and wet,
laid bare before your dazzling feet.

Freeze scars of pleasure
as you greet each rapture
from the crowd.
Forget desire,
draw chilling breath,
don't let emotion breach
the distance set
between sharp blades and ice.
Retreat ice maiden:
dance.

The curtain falls:
a rivulet of blood
seeps from the ice
as yet another encore rings
complete with my successor's name.
You meet.
You draw him to your rimy net
Ice maiden;
dance.

Hepplewhite Dresser

Filled with the wonder a child feels at Christmas,
removing the wrapper to find, hid inside,
the toy he had hoped for,
the gift he had longed for,
I found you, I bid, and I brought home my prize.

Charged with the strength of the groom at the threshold,
I carried you into the workshop of love.
The treasure I'd prayed for,
the pleasure I'd paid for,
a Hepplewhite dresser, now mine, to restore.

Blessed with the skill of an artisan's fingers,
gently abrading veneers of the past,
turning the years back,
holding the tears back,
the heart of the oak was revealed in the wax.

Drunk as the priest, on the law, at the altar,
synergy, evil, absolved by the chaste,
the life I abhor there,
the lies on the floor there,
twenty-five years of another man's dust.

Bathed in the splendour of God in his glory,
an old man's creation, pristine, restored,
waiting for me to
disfigure anew, to
embellish its frame in the style of my choice.

1. Across,
That Great Charmer
(Anag.)

Love, though lifelong, has to be renewed;
doubts overcome, to give illusion
to a constant, caring, state;

a series of short love affairs
re-embarked upon. We choose
the path we take. Today
I have reviewed my love
for you.

The magic's gone;
cracks begin to show.
I hear you still
amazon, queen
of all that you survey;
your venal words betray
the bond between us.

In the wake of your passion
you have left too many dead,
and I the same.

This is goodbye
and I must place my kiss
beside another's name.

A Lassie From Liverpool

Keep your sport of kings
your champagne toasts, and midget men
who cling to fillies' manes;
fly from the stalls into five furlongs
worth of bashing balls to bring
a highbred maiden's dripping loins
towards the winning post.

No, keep your sport of kings.
Give me the long race,
race of strong hearts
where eighteen throbbing hands
will drag me, breathless,
round three circuits of the track.

Strap me on a chestnut mare
whose crop-scarred flanks bear witness
to the countless men who jockey
for position as she dares to tease
the breath of twenty stallions
stabbing at her rear;
comes to the front
then comes again with no holds barred
ears pricked and nostrils flared
across the line
a length in hand with still
a length to spare.

Cuddles

He called her princess;
tucked her in, tightly;
kissed her, lightly,
and called her princess.

Princess she was
and nightly, bejewelled;
bedecked with chiffon dresses;
spinning, dazzling, drowned
in soft caresses
she would danced
and he, entranced,
would call her princess.

He called her princess
and daily, after dark,
unclasped the box
until, at last,
with shaking hands
he touched her . . .

. . . and clad
in nothing more than secrets
she would dance
and he
would call her princess.

He called her princess; now
he calls her whore.

Chicken Shit And Ribs

In ranks of plastered knees and rat tail hair
they sit in awe, awaiting older hands
to show them how to shape the twisted pile
of chicken wire into a wobbly frame.

. . . and layer, on layer, on layer, of stippled pulp
is pressed into the frame by jerky hands
that shake, and wait, impatient for the glue
to dry; then daub the thing with poster paint.

At the end of one creative term,
along with catapult and half-sucked sweets;
a glittering mosaic of three wise men;
he carries home his papier-mâché man.

Proud parents hold the paper man aloft,
singing his praises to a wondrous god
who made with them a covenant at birth:
a teacher's hand confirms that he'll go far.

. . . and far he goes, but always at his side,
transported in a tea-chest of his dreams
to reach its place on ever higher shelves,
the paper man: his conversation piece.

Once a year he takes it down to dust
a cobweb from the corner of its world:
he looks into the once bright-painted eyes
and crazy face of varnish, over-cured.

He sees the paper patch stuck on the arm
that could not bend, so broke beneath the weight
placed on the light and fragile-tissued flesh
by overzealous family and friends,

who fingered scars of pleasure on its back,
reminders of the day, when unaware,
he left the man unguarded on the floor:
playmate for an over-friendly cat.

He feels the nail he hammered through the foot
to give the sagging body extra grip
when heavy winds, let in by open doors,
whispered threats to blow it off the edge.

He stares into the faded poster paint
then hurls the festered body in the fire:
instantly the papier-mâché burns
and leaves behind the frame of chicken wire.

What's Left

I take what's left and clutch it tight;
cold fingers gripping in the night.
The crumbs the jackal drops, to tease
the lion, who would once with ease
hunt boldly, putting all to flight,
or stalk and kill for pure delight,
I pounce on in the failing light.
No longer taking as I please,
                            I take what's left.

So pathetic is my plight,
time has robbed me of my sight
and fear has brought me to my knees
to beg for life I once would seize.
Now that I've lost the will to fight,
                            I take what's left.

Cross Bred

He walks alone,
the great minority of one:
do with him as you will.

He is insanity
abroad amongst the bitten tongues.

He walks alone:
he does not steal
but strides with measured step.

Do with him as you will
he will not compromise:
just one half pace in front of death
he walks alone.

He cannot alter truth:
his head cannot be bowed.
Do with him as you will
he casts no stones.

Bearing his cross, amongst the crowd
he walks alone.

Do with him as you will.

Solomon In All His Glory

From the eyrie:
seals basking; surf caressing; white horse riding.
Seagulls soaring; dipping; diving.
Wooded hills, grey squirrels chasing.
River banks, the beaver building,
busy with his rearranging.

> Head against the wind and weather,
> swimming hard against the water,
> tilling stone to feed the litter:
> watch the wise man at his labour.

From the eyrie high above us
cast yourself into the gale,
ride the winds, rise above them,
catch the sunbeams painting rainbows.

Dive beneath the raging torrent,
body turning with the current,
flowing forward, never fighting:
teasing pathways, round the mountains.

We will reach the sea together,
meet the surf-caressing seals,
share with them the joy of living,
join them in their white horse riding.

For The Love Of A Good Woman

For twenty years he dug that bloody hole.
The same hole: different places.
Not anywhere; not where the fancy took him:
he dug 'to spec'.

One night he upped and walked out,
ambled down the road,
picked a spot,
laid flat,
stretched
and melted into the tarmac
as if to say,
'my turn'.

After twenty years, he wanted to be dug:
feel cold steel slice his body,
taut muscles work it in,
turning him,
tossing him,
broken earth
tamped,
trampled,
trod back into shape,
rolled.

Don't You Know

Acres? oh . . .
two thousand, six hundred
and, ehm, . . . thirty eight,
don't you know.
As far as the eye can see,
down across the valley,
my family have always owned the land.

One or two people, nearby,
most dairy fellows,
(my family have always helped them out,)
had a spot of bother,
what with one thing and another
so, we bailed them out y'know:
we bought their land.
We gave them jobs y'know:
but, ungrateful so and so's,
they left and went away;
they bit the hand.

Ah! look now, over there
that's young Jamie, don't y'know.
Good egg, what: (came down from up north)
said there was no work,
so he listened to the words
of wisdom that he heard,
and bought a bike.
He arrived here cold and hungry
one damp October morning;
we took pity on him;
now he tends the birds.

I cannot understand
what makes the blighters steal
from their neighbours,
say, they need our birds to
make a meal, feed themselves,
would you believe it . . .   .
back in my father's time,
(the sixteenth Earl, y'know)
they would not conceive it,
what a notion!
Everyone knew his place,
and would keep it.

Yes, as far as the eye can see,
down across the valley,
my family have always owned the land.
As far as the eye can see,
we own the grouse; the pheasants:
not so many years ago,
we owned the bloody peasants.

Fly-By-Night

They circle the house.
The car, waiting, beckons from the drive.

They move in:
knock; knock again.
We hide, hands pressed against the children's mouths.

At last, darkness falls:
cheated, glaring back, they move slowly down the street.
The car beckons from the drive.

We kick our way downstairs:
ten years, too heavy to carry, almost claw us back;
we make the door.
Vultures, buff manilla, squealing death,
pursue us down the path.
Curtain chinks take aim;
fingers scar the air;
the car beckons:
wills us on.

Dawn waits. They return..
Doors splinter as sombre morning breaks.
Noon: the house is raped.

    We skip to the beach; laugh
    collect winkles for the kids' tea.

Away, somewhere,
Old Hawk's gavel hammers out the past:
the captive crowd, rapacious,
pick the bargains from our bones.

On Losing One's Direction

Raven legs:
black silk on waxen thighs,
jet seams in one direction;
vertical perfection.

Raven beak:
gold tip of predatory sighs,
points high with one direction:
perpendicular erection.

Raven skin,
stretched taut on painted chair,
soft spot has one direction:
horizontal connection.

Raven blood:
white wine on waxen thigh,
jet stream without direction;
premature affection.

A Heavy Tab

Escargots drip
long snail trails
of hot green butter
down my chin.

I sit in Angelo's spaghetti house
and ruminate,
remembering that first whore's kiss;
crème de menthe; Van Gogh;
first oyster, thrown back from the pit.
Acquired tastes
bought dear with lollipops;
sherbet dip, and Sandra Pigtails:
braced-toothed purveyor
of pre-pubescent bliss,
now pushed aside
as I trek
in search of Amazons
with thighs to grip
my neck
in one long kiss of clotted cream . . .
. . . an acquired taste.

A Bag Of Jewels

The heel digs deep,
earth gives way to a practised twist;
the hole is dug.

Pearls are cast.
They pay no heed as they stalk the green
with their turf scarred knees:
a band of men who will quickly grow
into tired boys who remember when
they would gamble all on a polished throw
and a finger flick of the cut glass runes.

But the time is now.
Leather rubs,
glinting white on a black brogue toe.
It's twenty up, the cup's near full.
A hush descends; only one to go.

Then the final shot,
the final click:
the final knell of the funeral peel.
The game is lost.
All is lost.
The boy is born of a broken heart.

Bella Donna

White canvas glares
back from the looking glass:
colourwash sockets; bedraggled locks.
On the dresser, her female mystery:
fairy queen; earth mother; Pandora's box.
Pencils to blacken
brows that are barren:
chemically conquered, lost without trace.
Roll-ons; spray-ons; lipsticks
that stay on wet lips
as they cling in an endless embrace.

An artist's impression
signed: self-satisfied.
Finishing touch is skin's counterfeit sheen
squeezed from a bottle, (thinking, lanolin)
her body smothered in vanishing cream.
Leaving me
physical: face pharmaceutical,
spiritual: sediment; cosmetic dream.

Socially Insecure

Wednesday morning, 9.15 more or less,
Expectant, I slide into the local office of the DHSS
Life's a mess.
Frozen faces, 37 hostile glares
Accuse my air of affluence amongst the battered wives and
broken chairs.

Robot stares,
Evidently suited to a morgue, dim

Slowly as the chilling tales unfold, of how the blue informers sing,
Terrifying,
An old scrounger into a heart attack.
The Giro gives a mocking smile, well, fifty pounds, you couldn't
live on that.

End of chat.

I Mean, You Have To Laugh

I watched.
A short life
and at the business end . . . death;
betrayal by oneself,
or friend:
an instrument of preordained demise
whose prize lies scattered
in the field.

We played our part.
The twelve of us
mingled with the crowd,
led the chanting,
calling out his name.
We assumed he'd be released:
he staked his life on it.
    Shame Barrabbas had so many friends.

I moved back behind the throng
afraid that he might somehow
infect me.
Don't get me wrong:
we all loved him
but once we knew he had to die,
then best he went alone.

I mean,
I'd already had a narrow escape:
some cretin in the village screamed,
I've found another one.
Me, I said, break bread
with a wanted man.
No. Not me. No.

We heard the cock
crowing in the morning:
it happens every day,
no way will they fall for it.

Mind you, we did have some fun:
upset a few Pharisees.
I wasn't aware until that day
how he could work the crowds.
(quite easy really - Lazarus was a great help)

Yes, we had a few bad times
but mostly good:
the food; the wine;
feasts at every stop.
Not like his cousin John,
I mean, look what he got
for all his trouble.

No, you have to hand it to Jesus:
he was the master.
Even at the end
when nothing could be done,
hanging on the cross
he raised his head and spoke,
'Forgive them Father . . .'

What a stroke.

Room 101

I lined a cardboard box
with silk; fed her
honeyed bread;
milk to restore,
until, terrified,
I tried to cage her.

I crossed the room
to kiss her
but found her
flown, wing intact;
bones knitted, she
grown too strong
for me -
too weak to keep her.

I crossed the room
and found her
flown, but
in whichever nest
she now reclines,
I ask her
please, to
think of me with fondness,
not regret,
as I sit alone and pick
at threads that dangle
from the remnants
of our love:
    a cardboard box;
    a square of silk;
    a pile of sparrow shit.

A Synergic Affair

Her leopard spots were hard to hide:
by accident, he found
inside the car
a box of matches from a hotel bar
'meant nothing.

Laddered stockings in the bin;
hurried baths
when she came in from work
meant nothing.

Withdrawals from the cash machine;
her snoring
when they could have been
fucking
meant nothing.

But, all together
with the Oral B;
the Femfresh;
and the three times in one week
the car broke down;
her business trips out of town;
the sleepy voice that called him . . . Phil?
her decision to go on the pill,
all this, meant something,

    and though she tried
    and though he tried
    her leopard spots
    were hard to hide.

Pass The Parcel

Behind grey walls the chairman
calls for order:
minutes agreed, the speakers proceed
to push around the table
the possibility that, maybe,
statistically, she could be
at risk.

Wispy trails of under-manning;
within the constraints of the budget;
slight interdepartmental misunderstandings
diplomatically weave
the day's conclusion.

Motion agreed, the members proceed
to seek their place of safety.

Behind grey walls another meeting
falls into disorder - lovers kiss
- hold hands and kick another broken toy
into a corner.

Pissed Again

I'm pissed again, the wit is out.
I s t a g g e r through another bout
of hazy bliss, on warm dark rum.
The edges smooth, the grey cells numb,
I'm easy prey, without a doubt
to t thless hags who vie to tout
soft goods to tease a drunken lout.
Tonight I'll sleep in any slum,
    I'm pished again.

Sobriety ish life without
the naughty bits. When it's my shout,
then call for sediment and scum.
Let's lick the plate and kiss the bum
Of life, and laugh at pox and gout.
    I'm pis
        s
           e
             d
                  ag
                    a
                      i
                         n

Premium Life

'I can't face the rest of my life,'
the insurance man quietly pronounced.
He leant on my shoulder;
slowly grew bolder,
till finally, tight, he announced:
I'm considering leaving my wife.'

He dreamt of the army that night;
of brave deeds that had won a man's heart;
of the children who died;
the parents that cried,
till finally, tight, he announced:
'I'm considering leaving my wife.'

He paid all his dues and demands
to a woman who misunderstood
her potting shed major
who lived with such ardour,
till finally, tight, he announced:
'I'm considering leaving my wife.'

He threw himself clear of the loft.
The rope, it bit deep in his neck.
He hung in the hall;
no insurance at all,
till, finally tight, he announced:
'I've considered: I'm leaving my wife.'

Should I Save Up Seven Summers

Should I save up seven summers,
stuff them in a jiffy bag,
and with the strength that Hiawatha,
in the poem, flung his mother,
fling my package even higher.
Fling it all the way to Heaven;
fling it to the Pearly Gate,
fling it full of seven summers;
seems to be the going rate.

Would old Greybeard, with compassion,
bend his head to read my letter.
Bend his head and look with horror;
shed a tear for Man's oppression.
Shed a tear and watch it plummet,
to the depths of our despair?

The Curse

Mr Roy Fischer:
overpraised yet underpurchased
literary figure,
tonight holds audience before
the rapt ensemble
numbering, at least, twenty-four.

Polished, refined,
presenting well-worked passages,
no doubt, designed
to stretch a convoluted point
but not the mind.

With glacial quick wit
he moves from page to page
as we, (stifling shuffles,)
sit for an age,
one eye on Norman's coffee
(or his daughter's thighs,)
one on the sage
who postulates
the notion of the 'Tabloid Poet'.
(Page three will never look the same.)

Dying for a smoke, eventually,
we pass on to the only words
this deity wrote on sex;
I hope his experience surpassed
the feelings he evoked.

Poor Mr Fischer:
geriatric arsehole kisser,
passions buried in rehearsed gesticulation,
ideas aborted by some literary menstruation;
mere germs of life ejected to a publishing house cycle.

Toys In The Attic

It's raining,
about half-past ten,
I've parked the old princess on level six.
As I lock the door I se him walking,
slowly, from the other side.
Just an ordinary guy: average size;
mid thirties. Nothing unusual
except, to my surprise
he's wearing my jacket.

Black;
well-cut;
double breasted;
one hundred per cent
pure new wool: the jacket
I didn't buy last week.
The jacket
I lost on the toss of a coin:
heads, the jacket;
tails, the gas bill.
I flipped, watched the coin spin; stop;
hang in mid-air; fall.

Funny thing that gas bill:
first bill I ever paid
before the red.
I thought that I'd be chuffed,
instead, it left me drained.

'Thank you,' the 'glasses' said:
stamped it; initialled it, slid it
back across the desk.
I shuffled from the showroom;
took me back to when I was a kid, and
my first brush with philosophy.
'Nothing's impossible,' my old man said.

Lift yourself off the floor
using your bootlaces: that's the one
that niggled me.
I tried, in secret, year after year;
even on the gas bill morning
I poked my fingers
through the loops and gave it
all I'd got: nothing moved.
Like refusing to pay
the poll tax; in the end
you lose.

Even level six is a rebellion:
straight for the top, no messing
about at the bottom, cursing,
waiting for someone to die
at the wheel;
give up his spot.

I walked towards the yellow door marked 'Exit':
the jacket walked my way.
We drew together' a movement
of the eyes: that look. The look
existing only if returned. I returned
his look; my face
his mirror.

It doesn't happen often: maybe
in a pub; at a party: a look that draws
speech. 'I know you, from somewhere,'
'have we met, before.' Anything
to break the look. Succumb, and something
happens; has to happen:
so we nod; speak;
look away;
anything to break the spell:
anything but pay the bill;
anything but touch.

We looked away:
he to the side;
I looked downwards.

I stopped at the yellow door,
hand on the metal handle.
. . . Odd; out of gear; does not compute:
level six;
empty;
my car;
me;
level six;
empty;
straight to the top;
him.
I turned, the jacket, back to me, kept walking:
did not stop; did not hesitate.
I heard him hit
the headlines.

'Shit,' that's all I said,
just 'shit.'

Through the doors the lift waited: his lift,
empty; gleaming steel; rows
of black buttons;
a big green arrow, flashing:
'going down'.
I took the stairs.

I spun the shopping
into four hours: sat awhile
in McDonald's
not wanting to go back:
last to see him alive.

What could I tell them? - I looked
into a stranger's eyes
and loved him.

I retrieved the car but didn't
go to town for five more months:
gas board again.

I queued for 'glasses',
among the coughs
and walking frames, and when I stood
up front, I slipped a hand into my
well-cut; black; pure new wool
jacket,
took out the bill;
the final reminder;
the disconnection notice.
'I believe these belong to you,' I said
and dropped them on the desk.

I took the lift to level six;
walked through the yellow doors, marked 'Exit'.
A guy was locking up
an old princess, metallic blue, X reg.

As we passed, just for a moment,
our eyes met. We looked away but
I swear I heard him say:
'That bastard's wearing my jacket.'

Crowing

As I aspire
to acquire
the necessary ability
to give me credibility
as a bard
I pick up my pen and write
'Old crow sits on the creaking gate.'
    Wonder if I'll become
    the Poet Laureate?

www.ingramcontent.com/pod-product-compliance
Lightning Source LLC
Chambersburg PA
CBHW070108070426
42448CB00038B/2190